Braves in Beantown

A Century of Boston Baseball

Written by: **Alvaro P. Sanchez**

Copyright © 2025 by Alvaro P. Sanchez

All rights reserved.

This book or any portion thereof may not be reproduced or used in any manner whatsoever without the express written permission of the publisher except for the use of brief quotations in a book review.

Table of contents

Introduction
The Early Years (1871-1900)
The Golden Age (1901-1914)
The Struggles and Resurgence (1915-1930)
The Braves' Championship Years (1940-1950)
The Move and Final Years in Boston (1950-1953)
The Braves' Legacy
The Impact on Boston and Beyond
Conclusion
Appendices

Introduction

Boston. A city built on history, a city where baseball isn't just a game—it's a heartbeat. But for all the teams that came through, none left quite the mark like the Boston Braves.

In the early years, the Braves weren't just a team—they were the city's pride, a symbol of resilience and hope. From the time they first played in 1871, through their rise as the Beaneaters, and their eventual place in National League history, the Braves captured the hearts of fans.

It wasn't just about the ballgame—it was about family. It was about community. And it was about a city that loved its team with everything it had.

For much of its existence, the Boston Braves were a force to be reckoned with. They were one of the most dominant teams of the late 19th century, winners of multiple National League pennants, and home to some of baseball's earliest superstars. Their legendary 1890s dynasty saw them claim five pennants in nine years, setting the standard for excellence.

But the story of the Braves wasn't all sunshine and glory. There were years of struggle, seasons where the team could barely keep its head above water. Yet through it all, there was a loyalty from the fans that never wavered.

The team's ups and downs mirrored the story of Boston itself—gritty, unyielding, and determined to come out on top. In 1914, they shocked the baseball world as the Miracle Braves, pulling off one of the greatest comebacks in history to win the World Series.

And then came 1948.

That was the year when the Braves finally came close to glory. The team fought tooth and nail to claim the National League pennant, but even with the city behind them, the ultimate prize remained just out of reach.

But it wasn't the championship that defined the Braves. It was the energy, the passion, and the way the team brought people together. For those who lived through it, the memories of Braves Field and the sounds of the crowd are forever etched in their minds.

But life had other plans.

In 1953, after years of struggle and triumph, the Braves left Boston. They packed their bags, left Braves Field behind, and moved to Milwaukee. It was the end of an era, and for Boston, it felt like losing a part of itself.

Even as the Braves left, their spirit remained. For the fans who had stood by them through thick and thin, the Braves were more than just a team—they were family. And no matter where they went, the love for the team remained.

In this book, we'll revisit those years. We'll walk through the triumphs, the heartaches, the moments that made the Boston Braves so unforgettable. From their early days to their rise in the 1940s, through to their departure in 1953, the story of the Boston Braves is a tale of passion, perseverance, and love for the game.

For longtime baseball fans, this is a chance to rediscover the history of a team that helped define the sport. For newer generations, this book serves as a reminder that Boston's baseball history is about more than just Fenway Park and the Red Sox—it's about a team that once ruled the city, a team that left, but whose impact never faded.

The Boston Braves may no longer play in Beantown, but their legacy is still alive. Let's step back in time and relive the century-long journey of a team that once made Boston the home of two great baseball teams—before it became a one-team town.

Chapter One

The Early Years (1871-1900)

Baseball wasn't always the polished, corporate sport we know today. It started in small towns, with rough patches of grass and makeshift teams. And in 1871, Boston was right in the thick of it.

The city wasn't yet known for its championship culture, but something was brewing. A group of baseball enthusiasts had an idea—to form a team that could compete with the best in the country. So, the Boston Red Stockings were born.

This wasn't just any team. The Red Stockings were part of the National Association of Professional BaseBall Players (NA), the first professional baseball league. In 1871, the Red Stockings set out to make their mark, joining the league in its inaugural season. They were a part of history, but not yet legends.

Early on, the Red Stockings were far from the well-oiled machine we would come to know later. They were a group of players, some from Boston, some from around the country, united by one thing: the love of the game. The National Association wasn't the most organized or stable league—teams folded, and the competition was uneven. But that didn't stop the Red Stockings. They were determined, and in their very first season, they finished near the top of the standings. It wasn't the championship they dreamed of, but it was a step forward.

The early years weren't just about the wins and losses, though. It was about building a foundation—a team that would not only play the game but would also start shaping the culture of baseball in Boston. They played at the South End Grounds, a stadium that would become their home for many years. It was a place where fans gathered, not just to watch the game, but to witness the birth of a team that would define the future of Boston baseball.

In the first few seasons, the Red Stockings were a team of unknowns, but they had something more powerful than just talent: ambition. And while their performance in the early National Association years wasn't always stellar, their potential was undeniable.

***

By the late 1870s, the landscape of professional baseball was shifting. The National Association, despite its early promise, was faltering. Teams were folding, and the competition was far from consistent. But where others saw instability, Boston saw an opportunity.

In 1876, the National League was born, and with it, a new chapter for the Boston Red Stockings. The team made the leap from the National Association to the newly formed National League, solidifying their place as one of the sport's top contenders. But with this transition came more than just a name change—it marked the beginning of a new era in baseball.

The Red Stockings' transition wasn't a smooth one. The National League had higher expectations and stricter rules. It was a more competitive environment, and the Red Stockings had to prove themselves all over again. But prove themselves they did.

The first few seasons in the National League were a mixed bag. The Red Stockings were still a solid team, but they weren't yet dominating. They finished with decent records, but they found themselves up against tougher competition. Despite the challenges, the Red Stockings were beginning to find their stride.

It wasn't long before the team rebranded, taking on the name "Beaneaters" in the late 1880s. The nickname, though strange to modern ears, actually had roots in the city's culture. It was a nickname given in jest, likely referencing the frugality of the Boston team, but it would stick for years.

The Beaneaters' reputation grew quickly during the late 1880s, and their play became more dynamic. Under the leadership of men like manager Frank Selee, they started to show what they were truly capable of. This was when the Beaneaters began to build their legacy. They weren't just contenders—they were becoming a team to be feared.

Players like Hugh Duffy, who would go on to have an outstanding career, brought fire to the team. His incredible batting ability helped lead the Beaneaters to some of their best seasons. Duffy, alongside other key players like Kid Nichols and Tommy McCarthy, brought the team to the front of the pack. The Beaneaters quickly became one of the most consistent teams in the National League, with strong performances season after season.

A notable achievement during this time was the 1891 season, when the Beaneaters finished with the best record in the National League. They didn't capture a championship just yet, but their dominance on the field was undeniable. The team had finally hit its stride, and Boston was beginning to see the fruits of their loyalty and belief in the Beaneaters.

In a city known for its intellectual prowess and determination, the Beaneaters began to embody those very traits. They were smart, strategic, and tough—playing not just for the love of the game but for the love of Boston.

Though the Beaneaters didn't achieve the ultimate success in terms of championships during these early years, their reputation and performance began to set the stage for what was to come. The National League had made Boston a permanent fixture in the world of professional baseball, and the Beaneaters were ready to carry that legacy forward.

***

In the early days, the Boston Red Stockings weren't just another team—they were a collection of baseball pioneers. And while the team wasn't raking in championships just yet, there were a few names and moments that made people take notice.

Take Harry Wright, for example. A name that would eventually become synonymous with the very foundation of baseball in Boston. Wright wasn't just the team's manager—he was the visionary behind it. A former player who had seen the game evolve, he brought discipline and organization to the Red Stockings. His leadership set the tone for what would become a team that wasn't just participating in the game—they were shaping it.

Wright's influence wasn't limited to just coaching. He brought with him a new style of play that emphasized strategy, conditioning, and, above all, professionalism. He was a man ahead of his time, and under his guidance, the Red Stockings started to look like more than just a collection of players—they started to play like a team.

Then there was the immortal George Wright, Harry's brother. If Harry was the mastermind, George was the star. Known as one of the first true superstars of baseball, George Wright was a shortstop whose defensive skills were unmatched. He could field a ball like nobody else, and his bat? Just as lethal. The kind of player who made fans come to the games early just to watch him warm up. George's combination of speed, skill, and intelligence made him a game-changer, and he became a key figure in the early success of the Red Stockings.

But the team's success wasn't just about one or two standout players. The Red Stockings had an all-star lineup, with guys like Al Spalding, who would later become a household name not just for his playing, but for his contributions to the sport's equipment and history. Spalding was one of the best pitchers of his time, and his presence on the mound helped establish the Red Stockings as a team to watch. He wasn't just a player; he was part of the foundation that would allow the team to grow into the powerhouse it was destined to become.

And then there were the games. Moments that would live on long after the final pitch. It wasn't just the wins, but how they won. The Red Stockings played a brand of baseball that was smart, fast, and tough. Fans came to watch not just for the outcome, but for the thrill of the game itself. It was during these early years that the seeds of Boston's baseball culture were planted.

But as much as the Red Stockings were a team of remarkable talent, they were also a team of remarkable moments. Moments that defined what it meant to be a Bostonian fan. The way they rallied together during tough games. The way the city seemed to hold its breath with every pitch. And, of course, the growing loyalty from the fans who began to see something special forming on the field.

It was these early years that set the stage for what was to come—the days when the Red Stockings would become legends, and Boston would become the epicenter of baseball greatness.

Chapter Two

The Golden Age (1901-1914)

As the 20th century unfolded, so too did the evolution of the Boston Beaneaters. No longer just a team scraping by in a competitive league, they were becoming a true powerhouse, and the baseball world was beginning to take notice.

The dawn of the new century marked the Beaneaters' entrance into what many would call their golden age. They weren't just playing baseball—they were setting the standard. The 1900s brought a blend of great management, skilled players, and a surge of talent that catapulted the team into the upper echelons of baseball. The Beaneaters weren't just a team of the past—they were a team that was going to shape the future.

In 1901, under manager Frank Selee, the Beaneaters were making a statement. Selee, already a legendary figure in Boston, was a master of strategy and had the pulse of the team in his hands. Under his leadership, the Beaneaters played a brand of baseball that emphasized efficiency, precision, and defense. It wasn't flashy, but it was effective. The 1901 season saw the Beaneaters emerge as one of the top teams in the National League, and while they didn't secure a championship, their success couldn't be ignored.

But it wasn't just Selee's coaching that fueled the rise of the Beaneaters. The players themselves were stars in the making. Hugh Duffy, a name now etched in baseball history, was one of the cornerstones of the team's success during this period. A Hall of Famer whose batting skills were unrivaled, Duffy became the face of the Beaneaters. His ability to hit for average, his speed on the bases, and his overall knowledge of the game set him apart as one of the finest players of his time.

Duffy wasn't the only standout player in this golden era. Kid Nichols, one of the greatest pitchers in the history of the game, was in his prime during these years. Nichols' control and consistency on the mound made him a force to be reckoned with. His partnership with the team's strong lineup was vital to the Beaneaters' dominance in the league. Year after year,

Nichols delivered solid performances, proving himself as one of the best pitchers in the league.

Meanwhile, Tommy McCarthy, another key player, was dazzling on the field. His quick feet, sharp reflexes, and ability to get on base added to the Beaneaters' well-rounded success. As an outfielder, McCarthy was a key contributor to the team's offensive and defensive strength, playing a vital role in the Beaneaters' sustained excellence during these years.

The team's success during this era wasn't just about individual players—it was about cohesion. They weren't a group of stars who happened to be playing together; they were a team in every sense of the word. And as a result, they became a dominant force in the National League. By 1903, the Beaneaters had established themselves as a championship-caliber team, consistently finishing near the top of the standings.

The 1910 season was one of the high points of the Beaneaters' rise. The team posted a remarkable record and demonstrated the full potential of what they could achieve when every part of their game was clicking. Though they didn't secure the National League pennant, their performance that year solidified their place in baseball history.

It wasn't just about the wins and losses, though. The Beaneaters' success helped turn Boston into a baseball city. Fans began to fill the stands, and the team became part of the fabric of the community. The Beaneaters were no longer just a team—they were Boston's team, a symbol of the city's resilience, pride, and love for the game.

As the years went on, the Beaneaters' dominance in the early 1900s continued to shape the history of baseball in Boston. They were laying the groundwork for the team that would eventually come to be known as the Boston Braves, and they were doing it with a combination of incredible talent, teamwork, and a passion for the game that could not be matched.

By the early 20th century, the Boston Beaneaters were no longer just a team on the rise—they were a cultural institution. Their success in the National League wasn't just felt on the field; it was felt throughout the entire city. The Beaneaters had become the beating heart of Boston's sports scene, and their rise to prominence brought the city together in ways few things ever could.

As the team's fortunes improved, so too did the passion of their fans. The stands at Braves Field were packed with people—young and old, rich and poor—who shared one thing in common: a deep love for the game and the team that represented their city. The Beaneaters were no longer just a part of the sporting landscape; they were woven into the very fabric of Boston itself. The fans didn't just cheer for the team—they lived and breathed every moment of the season.

In a city that had faced its share of challenges, the Beaneaters' success offered a sense of pride and hope. The early 1900s were a time of great change in Boston—industrial growth, population shifts, and social transformations. But through it all, the Beaneaters remained a constant, a symbol of stability and triumph. They gave the city something to rally behind, something that transcended the everyday struggles of life.

For many, the Beaneaters represented more than just baseball. They were a reflection of Boston's identity—a city that had long prided itself on its grit, its determination, and its ability to rise above adversity. The team's success on the field mirrored the spirit of the people who cheered for them. And with every victory, with every stunning play, the Beaneaters helped reinforce that spirit.

The team's dominance also made a significant impact on the local economy. As the Beaneaters' popularity grew, so too did the business surrounding the sport. Braves Field became a hub of activity, not just for baseball fans but for vendors, businesses, and local entrepreneurs. The success of the team meant more people coming to Boston for the games, more families filling the stadiums, and more businesses capitalizing on the excitement that the Beaneaters generated.

The Beaneaters' success was also a turning point for the way baseball was perceived in Boston. No longer was the sport just a pastime—it became a major part of the city's culture. It was a shared experience, a way for people to connect with one another, regardless of background or status. The Beaneaters were uniting the people of Boston, and they were doing it with style, determination, and the kind of baseball that made you proud to wear the city's name.

It wasn't just the locals who took notice—the national stage was watching too. As the Beaneaters became one of the top teams in the National League, they attracted attention from across the country. Their success raised the profile of Boston as a baseball city, and with every victory, they added another chapter to the city's storied baseball history.

One of the most lasting impacts of the Beaneaters' success was the way it inspired future generations. The team's rise through the ranks of the National League sparked an entire generation of players, coaches, and fans who would go on to shape the future of the game. The Beaneaters helped establish a culture of excellence in Boston, one that would influence not just baseball but all sports in the city for years to come.

The Beaneaters weren't just successful because of their on-field achievements—they were successful because they became a part of something bigger. They were a reflection of the city's soul, a team that represented not just baseball, but the spirit of Boston itself.

***

Hugh Duffy. The name alone speaks volumes. A Hall of Famer, one of the greatest to ever wear a Beaneater uniform. But Duffy wasn't just a player—he was the heart and soul of the team. His bat was a weapon, and his presence on the field could change the course of a game in an instant.

It wasn't just his power; it was his consistency. Duffy's ability to hit for average was unmatched. He knew how to make contact, how to place the ball where the defense wasn't. He wasn't just swinging for the fences; he was playing a game of chess with pitchers. Every at-bat was a carefully calculated move.

But it wasn't all about the numbers. Duffy had an infectious energy, a spark that electrified the team and the fans. He wasn't just a player on the field—he was a leader. He set the tone, pushing his teammates to elevate their game, to match his intensity. His drive was contagious, and it didn't stop with the bat. In the field, Duffy was a force, making plays that left spectators in awe.

Then there was Kid Nichols. The pitcher who could do it all. Nichols wasn't just another arm in the rotation—he was the cornerstone of the Beaneaters' pitching staff. His control was flawless, his ability to keep hitters guessing remarkable. Nichols was the kind of pitcher who could pitch a complete game and make it look easy. But it wasn't just about stamina. It was about strategy, and Nichols had it in spades.

His fastball? Untouchable. His curveball? Nasty. Nichols could change speeds like no one else, keeping batters off balance and unsure of what was coming next. He was a true artist on the mound.

And then there was Tommy McCarthy, the outfielder who seemed to do it all. Speed, defense, hitting—McCarthy had the complete package. He was the kind of player who could steal a base, rob a hitter of a home run, and hit for average all in one game. His versatility made him an invaluable asset to the team.

McCarthy wasn't just a piece of the puzzle; he was a key to the Beaneaters' success.

These players were more than just names on a roster. They were the reason the Beaneaters became a force to be reckoned with in the early 1900s. Each of them brought something unique to the team, something that set them apart. Whether it was Duffy's bat, Nichols' arm, or McCarthy's all-around play, they were the foundation on which the Beaneaters' success was built.

Their talent wasn't just recognized by their fans—it was recognized by the sport itself. These players didn't just play for the Beaneaters; they played for the history books. Their performances, their dedication to the game, and their passion for winning left an indelible mark on the National League.

The Beaneaters' golden era wasn't just defined by great seasons—it was defined by great players. Players like Duffy, Nichols, and McCarthy weren't just stars. They were legends in the making. And they helped carve the Beaneaters' place in history.

Chapter Three

The Struggles and Resurgence (1915-1930)

When the 1910s arrived, baseball wasn't just a game—it was a lifeline for many. But the world was changing, and no one knew how much the great conflict of World War I would impact the game. The Boston Braves, like so many teams, faced a series of challenges during this tumultuous time that would test the heart of the franchise.

The war was more than just a distant affair—it was a storm that swept through every corner of life in America. As men marched off to fight, the major leagues found themselves losing some of their most talented players to military service. The Braves were no exception. Star players were drafted, and many of them left the game behind, leaving the team vulnerable at a time when stability was needed most.

But it wasn't just about losing players—it was about the economic and emotional toll the war took on the nation. Baseball was a comfort, but it was also a reminder of everything the country was sacrificing. Attendance at games dropped as people dealt with wartime shortages, rationing, and the emotional weight of losing soldiers to the frontlines. For the Braves, and for all teams, this was a time of struggle—not just on the field, but in every aspect of the franchise's existence.

In the years following the war, the Braves faced the aftermath of the conflict. While many players returned home, the impact of the war lingered. The loss of key players, combined with the financial strain of the war years, left the team scrambling to regain its footing. The roster was depleted, and the coaching staff struggled to pull together a competitive team. The magic of the Beaneaters' golden years seemed a distant memory, as the Braves found themselves at the bottom of the standings.

But even in the midst of their struggles, there was hope. There was always hope.

The 1920s brought with them new challenges, but also a new beginning for the Braves. In a way, the struggles of the 1910s had hardened the team. They had learned how to survive, how to adapt. And as the world slowly recovered from the ravages of war, so too did the Braves. It wasn't going to be an overnight recovery, but it was a start.

The Braves' fortunes didn't turn on a dime—it was a slow climb back to competitiveness. The team had lost its star power, but there was new talent waiting to step up to the plate. Some of the players who had been on the periphery of the Braves' roster during the war years began to find their stride. New faces brought energy, and as the league itself began to heal from the war's disruption, the Braves found a foothold again.

Yet, the scars of the war era remained visible. While the Braves were no longer an immediate contender, the foundation had been laid for a future resurgence. The challenges of the 1910s hadn't broken the Braves—they had reshaped them, making them a team more resilient, more determined, and more ready for the battles ahead.

It was a time of rebuilding. Players like Jimmy Johnston, who joined the Braves in the mid-1920s, began to provide some stability. Johnston's bat was a welcome addition, and his leadership in the infield helped solidify the team's defense. While he wasn't a flashy player, his consistency was exactly what the Braves needed in a period marked by uncertainty.

The Braves, though still in the shadows of the larger teams in the league, were beginning to show glimpses of the potential they had once displayed. They weren't there yet—not by a long shot—but the foundations were being laid for a new era of Braves baseball. It was a time of gradual improvement, where the focus wasn't on flashy championships but on steady progress. The Braves had learned, much like the country itself, to adapt and survive. It wouldn't be long before that resilience paid off.

The aftermath of World War I and the struggles that followed would define the Braves for years. But in the 1920s, the seeds of something greater were being planted. The team was no longer just trying to hold on—it was beginning to set the stage for the next chapter in its history. And that next chapter? It was coming.

***

The 1910s and early 1920s weren't exactly kind to the Boston Braves. Their struggles on the field were made worse by a lack of star power, financial troubles, and the lingering effects of the Great War. The team wasn't dominating the National League like they once had, but it wasn't for lack of effort.

Despite the struggles, the Braves had a few players who shone through the murk of mediocrity, holding the team together and giving the fans a glimmer of hope. These players became the backbone of the franchise during a period when things seemed uncertain.

One such player was Les Mann, an outfielder who joined the Braves in 1920. Mann was never going to be the biggest star in the league, but he had something the Braves desperately needed during those tough years: consistency. He wasn't going to wow anyone with home runs, but he was reliable, able to hit for average and get on base at a steady clip. His play in the outfield, though not flashy, was solid—he was the kind of player who could get on base and make things happen when his team needed it most.

Another key figure during this period was Rabbit Maranville, one of the best shortstops in baseball history. Though Maranville had a slightly uneven stint with the Braves in the early 1920s, his eventual return to the team in the mid-'20s brought a much-needed spark. Maranville wasn't just known for his glove—though his defense was legendary—but for his spirit and leadership. He had a way of getting under the skin of opponents, but also inspiring his teammates to give more than their best.

His tenacity on the field and his natural ability to lead made him one of the most valuable Braves during the turbulent years. The Braves' struggles weren't solely because of a lack of talent—they had talent, but it was often scattered and inconsistent. With a player like Maranville, the team began to piece together the building blocks of something stronger.

However, the struggles of the Braves during this period weren't just about the players—they were about staying competitive in a rapidly changing league. The National League was growing, and teams like the New York Giants, Chicago Cubs, and Philadelphia Phillies were all improving. The Braves needed to find a way to stay competitive, not just in the short term, but over the long haul. Their finances were tight, and their ability to recruit top-tier talent was limited by both budget and the growing appeal of other teams.

The Braves did their best to stay afloat by focusing on homegrown talent and small-time trades. They didn't have the luxury of big-name free agents or blockbuster signings, but they had grit. The kind of grit that can't be measured in statistics.

While the Braves weren't quite the powerhouse they once had been, players like Eppa Rixey helped steady the ship on the mound. Rixey was a consistent starting pitcher who kept the Braves in games, even when the odds seemed stacked against them. His control and composure on the mound made him an asset during the most difficult of seasons.

Despite the occasional star showing, the team still struggled to break into the upper ranks of the National League. The roster was plagued by inconsistent performances, a lack of depth, and a string of bad seasons that kept them from truly contending. For every Rabbit Maranville or Les Mann, there seemed to be a season that slipped through their fingers.

But there was an undeniable hunger on the part of the players—a refusal to let the team fall into obscurity. While the rest of the league may have been looking at the Braves as just another also-ran, the players knew something that others didn't: the tide was about to change.

Though the Braves couldn't compete with the biggest stars of the league, they still fought tooth and nail. They were a team defined by heart, and it was that heart that would eventually drive them back to the top.

The 1920s were a rebuilding phase for the Braves, but it was also a time of transformation. The team wasn't just looking for the next star—it was searching for the right combination of grit, determination, and skill that could bring them back to prominence. The pieces were slowly falling into place. And the Braves were starting to get ready for their resurgence.

***

By the time the 1920s rolled around, the Boston Braves were due for a change. The decade before had been full of struggles, but the foundation was being laid for something bigger, something more competitive. The Braves needed to make moves to rise from the ashes of their past misfortune, and that's exactly what they did.

The transformation began with key additions to the roster, each one adding a new layer to the team's capability. Players who could hit, pitch, and defend—players who could turn the tide.

One of the first game-changers was Bob Smith, a pitcher whose arrival in 1921 gave the Braves a much-needed boost. Smith was a workhorse, the kind of pitcher who could eat up innings and keep the team in games, even when the offense wasn't firing on all cylinders. His consistency on the mound made him a reliable option for manager George Stallings, and he quickly became a crucial part of the Braves' pitching staff. It wasn't just Smith's pitching that turned heads—it was the sense of stability he brought to a team that had spent years in flux.

Alongside Smith was Pat Malone, another talented arm who strengthened the Braves' rotation. Malone was one of the more consistent pitchers in the National League, and his ability to control the game with his fastball helped stabilize the Braves' staff during the critical years of their resurgence. The addition of Smith and Malone gave the Braves a formidable one-two punch in the rotation—a far cry from the inconsistent pitching they'd dealt with in the years prior.

But the Braves' resurgence wasn't just about pitching. The offense was getting a makeover as well, and it started with a player who would go on to become one of the most important figures in the team's history: Rabbit Maranville. His return to the Braves in 1923 was nothing short of a turning point. Known for his fiery personality and unmatched passion for the game, Maranville brought a spark to the Braves' lineup that had been missing for years.

His impact wasn't just on the field; it was in the clubhouse, where he became the vocal leader the team needed. Maranville wasn't just a player—he was a firebrand, pushing his teammates to give their best every time they stepped onto the field. And it worked. With Maranville leading the charge, the Braves started to develop a winning attitude, something that had eluded them for so long.

Then there was Lave Cross, a veteran infielder who brought both skill and experience to the roster. His steady defense and bat were a welcome addition to the Braves' lineup. He wasn't the flashiest player, but he didn't need to be. Cross did the little things right, the kind of player who went unnoticed by many but was integral to the team's success.

With these new players in place, the Braves were starting to find their rhythm. The pitching staff was deeper, the defense stronger, and the offense more balanced. The team's chemistry was improving, and it showed on the field.

But the key to the Braves' resurgence was not just about talent—it was about a shift in mentality. The team began to play with a renewed sense of purpose, one that carried them into the 1923 season, where they finished in a respectable position in the standings. Though they didn't win the pennant that year, the Braves had firmly planted themselves back into the conversation of competitive teams in the National League.

The Braves' recovery wasn't an overnight success. It was a slow and steady climb, built on a foundation of hard work, new blood, and a shift in mindset. The 1920s were years of transformation for the franchise—a period that would set the stage for even greater success in the years to come.

And by the end of the decade, the Braves were no longer a team in decline. They were contenders again. They had weathered the storm, dealt with the aftermath of war, and had rebuilt their roster into a competitive, hungry team. The stage was set. And in the years ahead, the Braves were ready to remind the National League why they had once been among the league's most dominant teams.

Chapter Four

The Braves' Championship Years (1940-1950)

The 1940s marked the beginning of the most successful era in the history of the Boston Braves. After years of ups and downs, of rebuilding and struggling to regain their footing, the Braves finally seemed to put it all together. They not only became a dominant force in the National League but, in 1948, they reached the pinnacle of success—winning the National League pennant.

The 1940s were a time of transformation for the Braves. No longer were they the team battling to stay competitive; they had become a powerhouse, thanks to a combination of skilled players, brilliant management, and a fresh wave of enthusiasm that flowed through the team. The foundation for their success was laid in the early part of the decade, but it was the mid-'40s when everything clicked.

The 1948 season stands out as the high point of the Braves' championship years. The team's remarkable performance that year wasn't a fluke. It was the culmination of years of hard work, strategic planning, and the emergence of key players who could finally deliver on the promise of a championship contender.

The Braves were led by manager Billy Southworth, who took over the team in 1945. Southworth, a former player and experienced manager, knew what it took to win. His leadership was vital in turning the team around and getting the most out of every player. Under his guidance, the Braves became a disciplined, competitive team, setting the stage for their successful 1948 season.

Key players like Eddie Stanky were central to the Braves' success. Stanky, a fiery second baseman, was not just known for his ability to get on base but also for his leadership. His relentless work ethic and passion for the game rubbed off on his teammates, and his role as a catalyst in the Braves' lineup became undeniable. Stanky wasn't the flashiest player on the field, but his contributions—both offensively and defensively—were crucial to the Braves' rise to the top.

Another critical piece of the Braves' success in the late 1940s was Johnny Sain, a pitcher whose talent helped solidify the team's pitching staff. Sain, who had come over from the St. Louis Cardinals, was a major factor in the Braves' pennant run in 1948. His consistent pitching throughout the season gave the Braves the stability they needed on the mound. Alongside Warren Spahn, who was also having a career year, the Braves had one of the best pitching rotations in baseball. Spahn, the workhorse of the staff, was at the peak of his career, and together with Sain, they formed an outstanding one-two punch that kept the Braves competitive all season long.

By the time the Braves reached the final stretch of the 1948 season, they were in a tight race for the National League pennant with the Brooklyn Dodgers and the St. Louis Cardinals. The final games of the season were filled with drama, as every pitch and every play seemed to matter. But the Braves, bolstered by Stanky's leadership and the brilliance of their pitchers, held their ground and secured the pennant, clinching the title on the final day of the season.

The Braves' 1948 National League pennant win was an attestation to the team's resilience and determination. It wasn't just about talent—it was about believing in the process and trusting that the team had what it took to make it to the top. The Braves had fought through years of struggle, but in 1948, they were finally able to capture the ultimate prize in the National League, sending their fans into a frenzy of celebration.

However, their World Series dreams were dashed when they faced the Cleveland Indians in the World Series. Despite an impressive effort, the Braves fell short, losing the series in six games. The loss was a crushing blow for the team and their fans, who had hoped for the World Series title to cap off an unforgettable season. But the Braves' performance in the 1948 season still stands as one of the greatest achievements in the team's history. They had gone from a team fighting for relevance to National League champions—and for that, they would forever be remembered.

While the Braves' World Series appearance in 1948 was the crowning moment of the decade, the entire era of the 1940s marked a period of resurgence for the team. The Braves had once been a struggling franchise, but by the late 1940s, they were once again a force in Major League Baseball. Their National League pennant win in 1948 wasn't just a triumph on the field—it was a reminder of the team's ability to rise above adversity and reclaim their place among the best.

The 1940s also saw the team reinvigorating its fanbase, who filled Braves Field to capacity as they cheered on their team. For the first time in decades, the Braves were contenders. The team had shed its former image as a lackluster club and had become a symbol of Boston's baseball pride once again.

The success of the Braves in the 1940s set the stage for the next chapter in the team's history, one that would ultimately lead to their relocation to Milwaukee in 1953. But for those who lived through the 1948 season, the memories of that year—of the Braves' incredible run to the pennant, their near-miss in the World Series, and their lasting impact on the city of Boston—will never fade.

***

As the 1940s unfolded, one player stood at the forefront of the Braves' quest for greatness: Eddie Stanky. A fiery, relentless competitor, Stanky was more than just a second baseman—he was the heartbeat of the team. His leadership, both on and off the field, played a pivotal role in the Braves' rise to the top of the National League.

Stanky was known for his ability to get under the skin of his opponents. He wasn't afraid to play the mental game, using his sharp wit and aggressive play to throw off opposing teams. His reputation for being a scrappy, hard-nosed player made him a fan favorite in Boston, and his competitive nature set the tone for the rest of the Braves' roster.

But it wasn't just his fiery attitude that made Stanky invaluable. He was a catalyst in the Braves' lineup. His ability to get on base—whether by hit or by drawing walks—was crucial to the team's offense. Stanky's on-base percentage in 1948 was among the highest in the league, and his presence on the field forced opposing pitchers to alter their strategies. He wasn't just a player—he was a symbol of what the Braves had become: a tough, relentless team that would fight for every inch.

Off the field, Stanky's leadership was equally important. He helped foster a winning attitude that permeated the entire clubhouse. Players like Johnny Sain, Warren Spahn, and Bobby Thomson looked to him for guidance, and Stanky's refusal to accept anything less than their best raised the collective level of play. The Braves were no longer just a group of players—they were a unit, driven by a shared purpose.

The impact of Stanky's leadership couldn't be overstated, especially as the Braves' quest for the World Series loomed in 1948. The team's remarkable run to the National League pennant was due in no small part to Stanky's contributions. He didn't just lead by example on the field—he inspired his teammates to perform beyond their limits, rallying them to push forward even when the odds were against them.

The Braves' road to the World Series, however, wasn't easy. The National League was stacked with competition, and the team faced tough opponents at every turn. The Braves entered the 1948 season with high expectations, but that didn't guarantee success. The race for the pennant was filled with tense moments, especially against the Brooklyn Dodgers and St. Louis Cardinals, two of the most formidable teams in the league at the time.

But Stanky and his teammates didn't flinch. They fought tooth and nail, never backing down from the challenge. When the Braves clinched the National League pennant on the final day of the regular season, it was a moment of triumph that felt years in the making. The Braves, once a team on the brink of collapse, had finally reclaimed their spot among the best in baseball.

The excitement was palpable in Boston as the Braves prepared to face the Cleveland Indians in the World Series. The Braves had come so close—just one final hurdle separated them from championship glory. But the Indians, led by the likes of Lou Boudreau, Bob Feller, and Satchel Paige, were no slouches. The series would prove to be an intense, high-stakes battle, with each game bringing its own drama and tension.

The Braves fought valiantly, but in the end, they fell short. Despite Stanky's leadership and the brilliant performances of players like Johnny Sain and Warren Spahn, the Braves lost the World Series in six games. The heartbreak was real, and the sting of the loss lingered long after the final out. But the Braves' 1948 season was not defined by that defeat—it was defined by the journey. The team had fought through adversity, had overcome the challenges of the past decade, and had reclaimed their place among the elite teams of Major League Baseball.

Though the Braves didn't win the World Series, their effort in 1948 was a reminder of what they were capable of. The team had come so far in such a short time, and they had proven that they were a force to be reckoned with. For the fans who packed Braves Field that season, the memories of those games, of the excitement and energy that filled the air, would live on forever.

In the years that followed, the Braves would struggle to maintain the same level of success. But the impact of the 1948 season—the leadership of Eddie Stanky, the resilience of the players, and the pride of a city behind them—would continue to resonate. The Braves' fight for the World Series in 1948, though ultimately falling short, marked the final chapter of the team's golden era in Boston. And for those who had witnessed it, the memories of that year would never fade.

***

When the Braves were winning in the 1940s, Boston wasn't just cheering for a baseball team. They were cheering for themselves.

The Braves gave the city something to believe in. After the war, after the hard years, there was a team that stood tall, a team that made the impossible seem possible. For the first time in years, the people of Boston had a reason to gather, to celebrate, to dream.

Braves Field was electric. The stands were packed, the air thick with excitement. Every game was a party, every victory a reason to shout. It wasn't just about baseball—it was about the pride of a city. When Eddie Stanky hustled, when Warren Spahn pitched, when the Braves fought, the whole city felt it.

Baseball became more than a game—it was a chance to escape. A chance to feel something bigger than yourself. The Braves weren't just playing for themselves; they were playing for the people of Boston. The fans didn't just watch the Braves—they lived the victories, the near-misses, and the heartbreaks.

For a brief moment, Boston wasn't just a city in New England—it was a baseball town. The Braves reminded them of who they were: tough, proud, and relentless. And though the team eventually moved away, the memories of that 1948 season, of the electric atmosphere at Braves Field, never faded.

The Braves didn't just leave behind a baseball legacy. They left behind a cultural mark, a reminder that when a team wins, so does the city.

Chapter Five

The Move and Final Years in Boston (1950-1953)

By the early 1950s, the winds of change were blowing hard in the world of baseball. The Boston Braves, once a powerhouse in the National League, found themselves struggling to keep up—not just with the competition on the field, but with the financial pressures and shifting dynamics of the city.

In 1953, after years of uncertainty, the Braves made a decision that would forever change the landscape of Boston baseball. They were leaving. Heading west. The city that had once embraced them would no longer be their home.

The decision to move to Milwaukee wasn't made overnight. It wasn't just about poor performance or fading fan support—it was about survival. Braves Field, once a symbol of the team's glory, had fallen into disrepair. The fans, though loyal, were no longer filling the seats as they once had. The team was facing mounting financial struggles, and with Boston's other big sports team, the Red Sox, dominating the baseball scene, the Braves couldn't seem to catch a break.

Milwaukee, on the other hand, was a city on the rise. The Braves saw a fresh start, a place where they could rebuild. Milwaukee was a smaller, hungry market, and the Braves knew they could become the city's new baseball obsession. The promise of a new beginning was too great to pass up.

The move wasn't just a business decision—it was a gut-wrenching goodbye. For years, the Braves had been a part of Boston. The fans had stood by them through thick and thin. Now, they would be left to mourn the loss of their beloved team.

The announcement came as a shock to many. While the Braves had seen their fair share of ups and downs in Boston, their move to Milwaukee left a bitter taste in the mouths of fans who had been with the team through its highest peaks and lowest valleys. The city had hoped for a turnaround, a revival, but instead, they were faced with the reality that their baseball team was packing up and leaving.

For the Braves, it was a chance to restart. For Boston, it was the end of an era.

When the Braves made the announcement that they were leaving Boston for Milwaukee, it sent shockwaves through the city. For years, the team had been a part of Boston's fabric, and now, the unthinkable was happening. The Braves were packing up, leaving their loyal fans behind, and moving west.

As the final days of the 1952 season ticked down, Braves Field was filled with a mix of disbelief and sadness. The stadium, once a buzzing hive of excitement, now felt like a monument to what had been and what was soon to be lost. Fans poured into the stands, perhaps for the last time, clinging to the hope that maybe, just maybe, the team would stay. But deep down, they knew it was over.

The final moments in Boston weren't grand celebrations—they were bittersweet farewells. The fans had seen their team battle, win, and lose. They'd seen the Braves rise to prominence and fall into decline. And now, they were witnessing the end of an era.

In those last few games, Braves Field was filled with the echo of a once-legendary team, a team that had given everything to Boston but was now being taken away. The fans didn't just watch the game—they relived the memories. The glory years. The triumphs. The near-misses. It was the end of an emotional chapter, one that would never be repeated.

Public reaction was mixed. For some, the Braves' move was the final blow to their connection with the sport. The Red Sox were already firmly entrenched as Boston's baseball team, and many fans saw the Braves as just another team that had let the city down. But for others, the departure was a betrayal. These were the fans who had supported the Braves through thick and thin, who had filled the stands during the 1948 pennant run, and who had believed that the team was part of the city's identity.

The Braves' departure was more than just the end of a franchise—it was a fracture in the heart of the city. Boston had become a two-team town, and now, the Braves were gone. The sense of loss was palpable. The feeling of abandonment hung heavy in the air, and no amount of fanfare could erase the bitter taste that lingered.

The last game in Boston, played in September 1952, was a melancholy affair. Braves Field, once alive with excitement, was now a quiet reminder of what had been. Fans clung to their memories, holding on to the hope that someday, perhaps, the Braves might return. But deep down, they knew that the team was leaving for good. And as the final out was recorded, the stadium grew still, a quiet reflection of what had been lost.

The departure wasn't just about a team leaving—it was about the end of a relationship. The Braves were no longer just a baseball team; they had become a part of Boston's identity, and now they were gone. The fans, left with nothing but memories, had to face the reality that the Braves were moving to Milwaukee, where they would begin a new chapter, leaving behind a city that had loved them for so long.

***

The final years of the Boston Braves weren't filled with the excitement and success of their earlier glory days. Instead, they were marked by a steady decline that mirrored the team's struggles both on and off the field. What had once been a proud franchise, a symbol of Boston's baseball identity, now seemed like a team adrift, unable to recapture the magic of its past.

In the early 1950s, the Braves found themselves caught in a storm of financial troubles, poor performance, and dwindling fan support. Their once-proud roster was no longer filled with the stars who had brought them to prominence. Players like Eddie Stanky, Johnny Sain, and Warren Spahn—the heroes of their golden years—had either moved on or were past their prime. The new players simply couldn't fill their shoes, and the Braves found themselves struggling to put together a competitive team.

Attendance at Braves Field, once a regular sellout, began to dip. The excitement that had once filled the stands was replaced with apathy. Boston had become a two-team town, and the Red Sox were firmly in control of the city's baseball landscape. Fans began to turn their attention elsewhere, leaving the Braves to play in near-empty ballparks. The economic pressures mounted, and the team's finances became increasingly strained.

The Braves' on-field performance during these final years was a far cry from their earlier success. The team hovered at the bottom of the National League standings, rarely making an impact. Even in their best years during the early '50s, they struggled to stay competitive. The days of fighting for a pennant, of being a dominant force in the league, were long gone.

Despite all of this, there were still flashes of the Braves' former brilliance. Players like Sid Gordon and Sam Jethroe showed moments of greatness, but those moments were few and far between. The team's struggles were a reflection of everything that was going wrong: aging players, weak pitching, and a lack of cohesion that had once made the Braves so formidable.

The departure of the Braves was inevitable, but it was still painful for those who had seen the team at its peak. It wasn't just the loss of a baseball team—it was the loss of a symbol, a part of the city's identity. The Braves had been a fixture in Boston for over 80 years, and now, they were leaving. The city had been their home, but as the years wore on, Boston had become a place where the Braves no longer belonged.

By the time the Braves packed up and moved to Milwaukee in 1953, it was clear that their time in Boston was over. The team had gone from a National League powerhouse to a struggling franchise, and the city, once so loyal to them, had moved on. But even as they left, the memories of their golden years—of the 1948 pennant win, of the thrilling games, and of the players who had defined an era—would live on in the hearts of those who had followed them from the beginning.

The Braves' decline in Boston wasn't just about a team's loss of talent or a dip in performance—it was about the end of an era. The team that had once made Boston proud was now a shadow of its former self, fading from the city's baseball scene and leaving behind only memories of what had been.

Chapter Six

The Braves' Legacy

The story of the Boston Braves may have ended with their move to Milwaukee in 1953, but their legacy is far from forgotten. The team's impact on baseball, on Boston, and on the history of the sport itself is undeniable. They were part of the fabric of baseball in its formative years, contributing not just to the game but to the culture surrounding it.

The Braves' history is a story of resilience and reinvention. They were a team that rose to prominence, fell from grace, and then made a valiant attempt at a comeback, all while maintaining a level of loyalty and commitment that resonated with their fans. Even when their performance on the field waned in the final years, their place in baseball history was solidified.

In Boston, the Braves were a symbol of the city's working-class spirit. They played hard, they fought for every inch, and they made their fans proud. Even though the Red Sox became the dominant baseball team in Boston, the Braves' impact remained. For the fans who had lived through the highs of the 1940s, the memories of the Braves' championship years—especially the 1948 pennant win—would never fade. The team's brief but unforgettable success reminded the city of what it meant to be a baseball town.

On a broader scale, the Braves helped shape the culture of Major League Baseball. They weren't just participants in the sport—they helped define it. Their style of play, their emphasis on defense, and their hard-nosed, no-nonsense approach to the game became a model for future generations of players and teams. Their legacy is seen in the way modern baseball is played, with a focus on team-oriented strategies and a never-quit attitude.

The Braves were also influential in the way the game was marketed and enjoyed. Braves Field, with its grandstands filled with passionate fans, became a place where the city could come together and celebrate the game. It was a place where history was made, where rivalries were born, and where unforgettable moments unfolded. For the people who filled those stands, the

Braves weren't just a team—they were a part of their lives.

Though the team's time in Boston was ultimately cut short, their impact on the game of baseball cannot be overstated. The Braves helped pave the way for future baseball dynasties, both in Boston and beyond. The passion they stirred in their fans set the stage for the kind of baseball fandom that would continue to thrive for generations. Their influence on the culture of the sport is something that continues to be felt, even as the years go by.

And though the Braves may no longer be a part of Boston's baseball scene, the city's connection to them remains strong. The legacy of the Braves lives on in the memories of the fans who witnessed their rise and fall, in the stories passed down through generations, and in the very soul of the city itself. The Braves' story is as much a part of Boston's history as it is of baseball's.

The legacy of the Boston Braves isn't just in the stats or the championships they almost won—it's in the unforgettable moments, the players who defined the team, and the stories that still echo through the halls of baseball history. Even after the Braves moved to Milwaukee, the legends of their greatest players and their most memorable games continue to live on, passed down through generations of baseball fans.

Hugh Duffy, one of the greatest players to ever wear a Braves uniform, remains a towering figure in the team's history. His .440 batting average in 1894 still stands as one of the highest single-season averages in baseball history. His influence wasn't just in the box score, though—he was a symbol of what the Braves represented: excellence, consistency, and an unwavering commitment to the game. Duffy's name still holds weight among baseball historians, and for the fans who saw him play, his legacy lives on in the stories they tell.

Then there was Eddie Stanky, the fiery second baseman who was the heartbeat of the Braves' 1948 pennant-winning team. Stanky's leadership on the field was unmatched, and his ability to get under the skin of his opponents made him a fan favorite. His presence in the clubhouse was just as powerful as his performance on the field. He pushed his teammates to be better, and in return, they followed him through one of the most exciting seasons in Braves history. The 1948 season, full of promise and heartbreak, remains a defining moment for the Braves franchise, and Stanky's role in that journey is forever etched in the memories of the fans.

There are also the unforgettable games, like the dramatic final day of the 1948 season, when the Braves clinched the National League pennant in front of a raucous crowd at Braves Field. The tension was palpable, the stakes higher than ever, and when the final out was made, the stadium erupted in cheers that could be heard all over the city. For the fans who had witnessed the Braves' ups and downs for years, that moment was pure magic. It was a reminder that no matter the years of struggle, no matter the challenges they had faced, the Braves could still rise to the occasion.

One game that still lingers in the minds of Braves fans took place in 1948, when the team faced off against the Brooklyn Dodgers in a tense pennant race. The Braves' offense came alive in that game, and Johnny Sain pitched a gem, keeping the Dodgers at bay while his teammates built a lead that would secure a crucial win. It wasn't just a victory—it was a statement. The Braves weren't just fighting for the pennant—they were proving that they still belonged in the upper echelons of baseball.

But beyond the games and the stats, it's the stories that continue to keep the Braves' spirit alive. There's the story of Johnny Sain's miraculous comeback from injury in the late 1940s, when he returned to pitch some of the best games of his career. Or the legend of Warren Spahn, who would go on to have a Hall of Fame career but was already showing signs of his greatness during his time with the Braves. Spahn, known for his incredible consistency and control, was the anchor of the Braves' pitching staff during their best years, and his stories of dominance on the mound are still passed down by those who watched him perform.

Even after the Braves left Boston for Milwaukee, their stories continued to live on. In Milwaukee, the team had a new beginning, but for the people of Boston, the

Braves' legacy was never forgotten. The players, the games, and the stories all became part of the city's baseball history. The Braves may have left, but they had planted seeds that would continue to grow in the hearts of the fans who had followed them so closely.

Today, the names of players like Rabbit Maranville, Sid Gordon, and Al Spalding still resonate with baseball historians, and the stories of their time with the Braves are told in every corner of baseball fandom. The Braves may have moved west, but their influence on the game, on Boston, and on baseball fans everywhere remains undiminished. Even now, when fans talk about the great teams and players of baseball's past, the Braves are never far from the conversation.

***

The Boston Braves may have moved to Milwaukee, but their influence on both future generations of players and the city of Boston remains undeniable. Even after the team left, the Braves' legacy lived on in the hearts of those who had witnessed their rise, their fall, and their brief return to greatness.

For future generations of players, the Braves' approach to the game served as a model. Their gritty, no-nonsense style of play wasn't just about talent—it was about a relentless work ethic and an unyielding belief in the team. Players like Eddie Stanky, with his fiery spirit, showed that leadership could come from anyone, not just the stars. Stanky's ability to rally his teammates and inspire them to give their all was a lesson that would continue to shape future leaders in the game. His approach to baseball—playing with heart and soul—became a blueprint for many of the greats who followed.

Then there were players like Warren Spahn, whose longevity and consistency set the standard for pitchers in the years to come. Spahn's mastery on the mound, coupled with his ability to adapt and evolve through the seasons, influenced generations of pitchers who came after him. His career became the gold standard for pitching excellence, and the Braves' role in shaping his development is a crucial chapter in baseball history.

Even in their final years, the Braves influenced the next wave of stars. The 1940s Braves showed that a team built on both star power and gritty teamwork could rise to greatness. And though the team's decline in the 1950s signaled the end of an era, the lessons learned during the 1948 pennant race and the World Series battle with the Cleveland Indians were passed down to future generations of players, reminding them that success on the field doesn't come without struggle.

For the city of Boston, the Braves' influence never truly faded. Despite the arrival of the Boston Red Sox as the undisputed baseball team in the city, the Braves left an indelible mark on the city's sports culture. The memories of their victories, especially the 1948 pennant win, remained in the hearts of Boston's baseball fans, and their stories continued to be shared among friends and families.

As the years passed, the Braves' legacy continued to be a part of the city's identity. The community that had rallied behind them in the 1940s—the same fans who had filled the stands at Braves Field—now passed their love for the team onto the next generation. Even though the Braves had moved away, their spirit remained woven into the fabric of Boston's baseball history. The city had witnessed the highs and lows of the Braves' journey, and those experiences shaped the way Boston would view baseball for years to come.

The Braves' move to Milwaukee didn't diminish the bond between the team and the city. Instead, it deepened it. The people of Boston, who had once cheered for the team in the stands, now passed their admiration and affection for the Braves onto future generations of fans. Even as the Red Sox became the centerpiece of the city's baseball scene, the Braves' impact was still felt. For many in Boston, the Braves were not just a team that once played here—they were a part of the city's soul.

Today, when people in Boston talk about their love for baseball, the Braves' name still comes up. The team's legacy, their impact on the game, and their place in Boston's history are never far from the conversation. The Braves' story may have ended in Boston, but the lessons they left behind, the players they inspired, and the love they cultivated for the game of baseball continue to live on.

Chapter Seven

The Impact on Boston and Beyond

The Boston Braves weren't just a baseball team—they were a cornerstone of the city's identity. From their earliest days as the Red Stockings in the 1870s to their final season in 1952, the Braves helped define what it meant to be a Bostonian fan of the game.

During their time in Boston, the Braves gave the city more than just victories and losses—they gave them a reason to gather, to cheer, and to unite around a common love for baseball. The Braves were a part of the community, woven into the fabric of the city's history.

Boston, already a city of passionate sports fans, found in the Braves an outlet for its own resilience. At the heart of Boston's love for the game was Braves Field—a place where memories were made and legends were born. The Braves' success during their peak years in the 1940s gave the people of Boston something to rally behind, something that went beyond the daily grind of life. They were a symbol of Boston's underdog spirit—fighting, scrapping, and never backing down.

In a time when the Red Sox were struggling to find their own place in the city's sports scene, the Braves were able to carve out a niche of their own. Braves Field was more than just a stadium—it was a gathering place, a home for fans to share in the joy of a team that wasn't afraid to face adversity head-on.

As the Braves continued to grow in prominence throughout the early 20th century, they became ingrained in the city's culture. Their successes, particularly the 1948 pennant-winning season, helped define an era for baseball in Boston. But even as the Braves faced challenges and, ultimately, moved to Milwaukee, their impact on the city remained. The Braves' story was as much about the people of Boston as it was about the players on the field. For those who had witnessed the team's highs and lows, the Braves had become part of what it meant to be a Bostonian.

When the team left for Milwaukee in 1953, it was as if a piece of the city's soul had been ripped away. Fans who had poured their hearts into supporting the Braves were left to grapple with the loss, but they had something the next generation would carry on: a connection to a team that had given them everything it had, and more.

When the Braves left Boston in 1953, it marked the end of an era for the city. But it was just the beginning of something new. The team's move to Milwaukee would have a profound impact, not only on the city of Milwaukee but on baseball as a whole. It was a shift that reshaped the landscape of the sport, creating new fans, new rivalries, and a new legacy.

Milwaukee, a city known for its love of sports but without a major league baseball team, welcomed the Braves with open arms. The city, hungry for its own baseball identity, quickly adopted the Braves as their own. The team's arrival in Milwaukee transformed the city. It was a moment of rebirth, of excitement, and of possibility. The Braves weren't just a team—they were a source of pride for Milwaukee, and they became the focal point of the city's sports culture.

The transition wasn't without its challenges, of course. The Braves had to adjust to a new city, new fans, and a completely different environment. But in a way, the move to Milwaukee was a fresh start. The team was no longer struggling in the shadow of the Red Sox in Boston. Now, in Milwaukee, they were the team everyone rallied behind. The Braves filled County Stadium with crowds eager to support their new hometown heroes.

The move was also a catalyst for a significant shift in Major League Baseball. Milwaukee's passionate fan base helped ignite interest in baseball across the country, especially in the Midwest. The Braves' arrival demonstrated that baseball wasn't just for the big cities on the East Coast—it was a national pastime, beloved by fans across the country, no matter where they lived. And as Milwaukee embraced the Braves, it became a central hub for baseball in the 1950s.

But it wasn't just about the Braves' success in Milwaukee. The team's departure from Boston had lasting effects on both cities. In Milwaukee, the Braves sparked an explosion of baseball enthusiasm that would lead to the creation of one of the most beloved franchises in the sport—the Milwaukee Brewers. While the Brewers were an entirely different team in their early years, they inherited much of the spirit and identity the Braves had cultivated in the city. Even as the team changed its name and affiliations over the years, the Brewers remained linked to the Braves' legacy.

For Boston, the loss of the Braves left a gap. The city had to cope with the void left by the team's departure, and while the Red Sox filled much of the space, the memories of the Braves still lingered. The Braves had been part of Boston's cultural identity for decades, and their absence was felt. But in some ways, the Braves' departure helped shape the future of the Red Sox fan base—turning the team into the clear focal point of Boston's baseball scene. The city's identity as a baseball town was solidified, and though the Braves were gone, the passion for the game only grew.

Even as the Braves found success in Milwaukee, the shadow of their Boston years remained. The team's history and legacy lived on in the stories shared by old fans, the players who had played in both cities, and the sense of continuity that tied the two eras together. And for those who had followed the Braves in Boston, the memories of their time there would never fade.

The Braves' move to Milwaukee was a transformative moment for both cities and for baseball as a whole. It marked the beginning of a new chapter for Milwaukee, one that would be forever intertwined with the team's success and the creation of the Brewers. For Boston, it was a painful goodbye, but one that would leave a lasting impact on the city's love for baseball.

The Braves' departure from Boston in 1953 may have left a deep sense of loss, but it ultimately had a lasting impact on the city's relationship with baseball. Though the team was gone, the foundation they had built in Boston helped shape the future of the city's baseball culture, influencing not only the Red Sox but also the entire baseball scene in the region.

For one, the Braves' success in the 1940s proved to Boston that the city could thrive as a baseball hub.

Despite the Braves' decline in the 1950s, the memories of their championship aspirations and the excitement of the 1948 pennant still lingered in the city's consciousness. The Red Sox, while firmly established as Boston's premier baseball team, now had a competitive benchmark set by the Braves—a reminder of the energy that comes with a winning team.

The Braves' move also contributed to the broader understanding of baseball as a national sport. Before the Braves' relocation to Milwaukee, baseball was largely seen as an East Coast and urban sport, but their success in a smaller market like Milwaukee helped break down that perception. It proved that baseball could thrive in a variety of settings, and cities like Boston would begin to appreciate their connection to the larger baseball community even more.

As the years passed, the Braves' legacy persisted in Boston, not just in the memories of their fans but in the city's growing reputation as a passionate baseball town. The Braves had played an instrumental role in establishing the fanbase that would later support the Red Sox through thick and thin. The Red Sox might have been the city's main team, but the Braves had laid the groundwork for a generation of fans who knew what it meant to love a team. The intense loyalty, the ups and downs, the heartbreaks—all of it had been part of the Braves' legacy.

One of the most lasting effects was the connection between Boston and its ballparks. The Braves' departure did not end the city's love for the game—it was simply a shift. As the Red Sox began to dominate the Boston baseball scene, their own successes and challenges became deeply intertwined with the history of Braves Field, which would eventually give way to Fenway Park as the focal point of the city's sporting life. The stories of the Braves' time at Braves Field would be passed onto future generations, bridging the gap between past and present, and creating an unbroken thread in Boston's baseball history.

The Braves' time in Boston also helped set the stage for future teams and fan bases. The success of the Braves, particularly in the 1940s, proved to future players and fans that Boston was a city that could love baseball with unparalleled passion. The city's eventual embrace of the Red Sox after the Braves' departure was marked by this undying commitment to the game—a commitment that the Braves had helped foster during their time in Boston.

And while the Braves may have left for Milwaukee, the connection between Boston and baseball remained intact. The legacy of the Braves was always felt in the background—an important part of Boston's history, even as the city turned its attention to the Red Sox and other future developments in the sport. The Braves, though no longer in the city, would always be remembered as the team that once defined an era for Boston's baseball culture.

Conclusion

The story of the Boston Braves is not just a baseball story—it's a story of resilience, transformation, and the unbreakable bond between a team and its city. Though the Braves ultimately left Boston in 1953, their impact on the game, on the city, and on the generations of fans who followed them remains as strong as ever.

For over eight decades, the Braves were a fixture in Boston's baseball landscape. They gave the city its first taste of professional baseball, helped shape the National League, and produced some of the sport's most legendary figures. From the dominance of Hugh Duffy in the 1890s to the heroic performances of Warren Spahn and Eddie Stanky in the 1940s, the Braves were more than just a team—they were a symbol of Boston's fighting spirit.

Their departure may have been painful, but it wasn't the end of their story. In Milwaukee, the Braves found new life, and their success in the 1950s further cemented their place in baseball history. Eventually, they moved again, settling in Atlanta, where they became one of the most recognizable franchises in the sport. But no matter where they went, their origins in Boston remained an essential part of their legacy.

The Braves' time in Boston also played a role in shaping the city's enduring love affair with baseball. While the Red Sox eventually became Boston's singular baseball identity, the Braves had already laid the foundation. Their influence was felt in the way the city embraced its teams, in the loyalty of its fans, and in the deep sense of history that surrounded the game in Boston.

Today, the echoes of the Boston Braves still linger. Braves Field may be gone, but its spirit lives on in the memories of those who once filled the stands, in the stories passed down through generations, and in the knowledge that, for a time, the Braves were Boston's team.

This book is a tribute to that legacy—a reminder that though the team may have moved on, its history remains woven into the fabric of the game. The Boston Braves were more than just a baseball team. They were a part of Boston itself. And that is something that time will never erase.

Appendices

Key Statistics and Records

Most Wins in a Season: 102 wins (1898)

Best Winning Percentage: .705 (1898)

Most Runs Scored in a Season: 1,220 runs (1894)

Most Home Runs in a Season (Team): 138 home runs (1953)

Longest Winning Streak: 18 games (1891)

Longest Losing Streak: 18 games (1928)

Most Career Wins (Pitcher): Warren Spahn (356 wins)

Most Career Hits (Batter): Rabbit Maranville (2,316 hits)

Most Career Home Runs (Batter): Eddie Mathews (493 home runs)

Most Strikeouts in a Season (Pitcher): Warren Spahn (191 strikeouts, 1952)

Most Batting Titles Won: Hugh Duffy (1893, 1894, 1897)

List of Significant Players and Their Achievements

Hall of Famers

Hugh Duffy – 1894 batting champion (.440 BA, highest in MLB history)

Kid Nichols – One of the greatest pitchers of the 19th century (361 career wins)

Rabbit Maranville – Defensive wizard, played 23 seasons (2,316 career hits)

Johnny Evers – Legendary second baseman, won MVP in 1914

Warren Spahn – Winningest left-handed pitcher in MLB history (363 career wins)

Eddie Mathews – Power-hitting third baseman (493 home runs, 2,315 hits)

Tommy McCarthy – One of baseball's early speedsters and defensive innovators

Frank Selee (Manager) – Hall of Fame manager who led the Braves to dominance in the 1890s

Other Notable Players

Eddie Stanky – Key leader in the Braves' 1948 pennant run

Johnny Sain – Ace pitcher, known for his dominance in the late 1940s

Bob Elliott – 1947 NL MVP, consistent offensive force

Sid Gordon – Key hitter for the Braves in the late 1940s and early 1950s

Sam Jethroe – First Black player in Braves history, 1950 NL Rookie of the Year

Timeline of Major Events in Braves History

Early Years (1871-1900)

1871 – The Boston Red Stockings (later Braves) were founded as a charter member of the National Association.

1876 – The team joins the newly formed National League.

1883 – Renamed the Boston Beaneaters, beginning a new era.

1892 – Win their first National League pennant in a split-season format.

1894 – Hugh Duffy sets the MLB record for highest batting average in a season (.440).

1898 – The team wins 102 games, the best record in franchise history.

Transition Period (1901-1930)

1901 – The American League was established, creating competition with the Red Sox.

1912 – Renamed the Boston Braves.

1914 — The "Miracle Braves" make an incredible comeback from last place to win the World Series, sweeping the Philadelphia Athletics.

1923 — Move into the newly constructed Braves Field, the largest stadium in MLB at the time.

1928 — Suffer an 18-game losing streak, one of the longest in team history.

Struggles and Resurgence (1931-1949)

1935 — The Braves sign Babe Ruth for one final season before his retirement.

1940 — The team officially rebrands as the Boston Bees before reverting to Boston Braves in 1941.

1948 — The Braves win the National League pennant, led by Warren Spahn, Johnny Sain, and Eddie Stanky.

1948 — Lose the World Series to the Cleveland Indians in six games.

Final Years in Boston & Move to Milwaukee (1950-1953)

1950 — Sam Jethroe becomes the first Black player in Braves history, wins NL Rookie of the Year.

1952 — Attendance dwindles as the team struggles financially.

1953 — The Boston Braves move to Milwaukee, becoming the Milwaukee Braves.

Milwaukee and Beyond (1954-Present)

1957 — Win the World Series in Milwaukee, led by Hank Aaron and Eddie Mathews.

1966 — Move again, becoming the Atlanta Braves.

1995 — The Atlanta Braves win the World Series, keeping the franchise's championship legacy alive.

Made in the USA
Columbia, SC
25 February 2025